# Calm for I

A superhero's guide to understanding

feelings and behaviour

by

Julie Cullen

Steve Connellan

DEDICATION

For our children and grandchildren

# CONTENTS

# ACKNOWLEDGEMENTS

Special thanks to Bennet Cullen who was our youth consultant and the initial inspiration for some of the cartoons in this book.

Thanks to Kiri Lightfoot for review and advice.

Illustrations by Steve Connellan

# Introduction for readers

Here's a heads up on how to use this book. To be clear, it was <u>not</u> written by a psychologist. Actually, it was written by two health professionals who:

- felt frustrated by the very long textbooks written in a complex and often scientific style that advise parents and professionals on how to support children's  behaviour and …

- have a talent for taking complicated information and making it practical, clear and easy for kids to understand.

It's based on extensive research; reviewing studies and relevant literature; gathering expert opinion on children's behaviour, which includes guiding behaviour positively and cognitive behavioural strategies.

In fact, this book is written for our own beloved children and grandchildren, including our many friends who found it so useful that they have encouraged us to share the strategies more widely. This is a book to read <u>with</u> your children. We hope you get a sense when you read it of how many families share similar challenges and, in fact, this book is full of lifelong skills that can be useful for just about anyone of any age.

There's not just one strategy for each section, there are several, because we are all different. Try them and see what works best for your child.

# Chapter 1

## The Superhero Manual

**What if I told you that this book was full of super powers?**

**What if I told you that you had stumbled across a superhero's manual?**

**Would you look inside?**

**YES, because who wouldn't?**

**Who wouldn't want to learn awesome superhero powers?!**

Now, what if I told you that if you learn these powers it will help you to feel better, make friends, get in less trouble and be the best version of yourself?
How much would you pay for these awesome powers?!

$100                     $1000                     $1,000,000?!!!!!

Well guess what. Some things can't be bought.
Sometimes even superheroes have to work hard to get their powers.
But I know you can do it. And I know because this book is fun. And funny.
And sometimes stupid! ........................ Enjoy.

**I'm sorry. I think I missed something. What did you say this book was about again?**

Everyone has different challenges that they might need a bit of help with.

Our challenges can help us to be more understanding of other people's difficulties.

This book teaches skills for managing our feelings and behaviour.

And that… Affects… EVERYTHING !!!

Here are some examples of challenges that people may need to overcome.

First up there are 3 main rules that all people have to follow.

**1.** **Don't hurt yourself**
*(be kind to yourself)*

**2.** **Don't hurt others**
*(be respectful to others)*

**3.** **Don't damage property**
*(respect property)*

For children and adults there are consequences for breaking these rules.

# Chapter 2

## Feelings

To become a superhero, these are the
basic facts you need to know about feelings.

1.  **All feelings are OK**

    (some are nice and some are a little harder to tolerate).

2.  **Thoughts build up in our mind and these lead to feelings**

| A | B | C |
|---|---|---|
| EVENT | THOUGHT | EMOTION |

**Can't find a pencil** ⟶ **I bet someone stole it** ⟶ **Anger, resentment**

OR

**Can't find a pencil** ⟶ **Maybe I left it at home** ⟶ **Disappointed, puzzled**

Do you see? This example is all about losing a pencil but the feeling depends
on the thought.

**Sometimes when we feel SUPER UPSET we feel like we have to**

**DO SOMETHING!**

BUT WE DON'T

Your feelings can't hurt anyone unless you act on them.

Feelings are like waves – they come and they go.

Sometimes they might hang around for a little while but they will go.

Sometimes we just have to sit with an uncomfortable feeling and know it can't hurt us and it will settle down soon. This is accepting your feeling. When you ACCEPT your feelings they will settle down more quickly.

If we feel REALLY REALLY upset there are things we can do to help us tolerate the feelings until they gradually fade away, like those waves on the beach.

We need to choose ideas that help us cope, not ones that hurt us. Otherwise, in the long run we feel much worse.

Here is a HUGE list of things you can choose. Add your own at the end and tick your favourites.

If you are SUPER upset and you do one thing that doesn't work, don't give up, keep going, work your way down the list. Still upset? Then go back to the beginning.

- Count to ten

- Read a book

- Listen to music

- Make a nice snack and focus on eating it

- Have a drink

- Go for a swim

- Go for a walk

- Have a shower or bath

- Lie down and rest

- Make something/create something

- Snuggle up with a toy

- Write your feelings down

- Write a story or cartoon

- Hug someone who cares about you

- Talk to your mum/dad/aunty

- Draw a picture

- Spend time in nature

- Notice all the sounds or sights around you

- Do something nice for someone else

- Add your own ideas

-

# Chapter 3

### The Anger Chapter!

Sometimes when you are SUPER upset, the feeling is ANGER.

Everyone feels angry sometimes. It's OK to feel angry and it can be a really useful feeling. Anger can let us know when something is wrong and, if we are treated unfairly, anger can help us to stand up for ourselves.

**But** anger can be a very strong feeling that we have to learn how to manage, so that we don't lose control.

Some people like to hit pillows or go for a run if they're angry, and let the feeling out.  If we are really angry, to help us calm down, we might need to move away from the person or task that has triggered it.

But there are times when we can't do that or when we can manage feelings of anger with some simple breathing techniques.

Getting to know what your body feels like as you get angry can help you act quickly and calm down while you're still in control. Then you can avoid ALL SORTS of trouble.

Take a look at the 'Angermometer' on the next page and fill in **worksheet 1** to get to know how you feel when you're angry.

## The Angermometer

**5** You have lost control. You are shouting or hitting. You want to harm what you feel hurt you.

**4** You are mad and can't think clearly. You are coming close to saying or doing something you might regret.

**3** You are upset about something. It's hard to stop thinking about it. You might feel you need a break

**2** Something happened and it bothers you a little bit. But it's not too much of a problem and you can let it go

**1** Things are going well. Nothing bothers you.

## Work sheet 1: Anger

## What happens to you when you're angry?

Fill in the work sheet to learn more about anger.

What does your face look like?

What happens in your body?

What things do you say to yourself?

What helps to calm you down?

- 
- 
- 
- 
- 
- 

Anger can be a useful feeling.

Write down any ideas you have about how anger could help you.

- 
-

## Superhero toolbox 1

Strategies to help you calm down when you're really mad.

If you feel ANGRY you can use 'turtle breathing' to take a moment to calm down.

You can learn how to 'turtle breathe' – it goes like this …

# OR

If you need to calm down quickly and the 'turtle breathing' is too slow, you could simply try:

## 3 DEEP BREATHS

Consider everyone's feelings

## THINK

What is the problem?

What are my options?

## CHOOSE

 **GO**

How did that go?

There are lots of different strategies that you can use to help you calm down - try them and find out what works best for you. Maybe there's someone you trust and look up to who would tell you how they calm down when they're angry. Here are a couple of our favourite ideas that people have shared:

**Ari says**,

*"I use counting a lot. When I'm angry, I say to myself, I'm going to take 5 deep breaths and when I've finished I can make great decisions."*

**Suzy says**,

*"If I can't figure out my homework and I get really mad, I take one deep breath in, put my hand on my stomach and breathe out slowly, watching my hand move with the breath. I repeat this until I feel calmer. Then I can decide whether to try again or ask for help."*

# Chapter 4

## After you've calmed down

When you feel calmer we can look at the thoughts behind your feelings.

- If there's a problem, you can problem solve.

- If your thoughts are negative and making you feel worse, you can change them with positive self-talk. Sometimes it helps to see the bigger picture.

- Are your thoughts playing tricks on you? Get to know the thinking error that can upset you.

- Is there a behaviour you want to change? Thinking about the pros and cons of your behaviour can help you make wise decisions.

- Use a pause and think strategy before you take any action.

The next few chapters will explain how to learn all these skills.

## Problem Solving

Problems come in all shapes and sizes. Some are easy to solve and others much more difficult, but that doesn't stop us trying to solve them.

Learning good problem-solving skills will help us to make good decisions and become the best version of ourselves.

Here's how to do it. When you feel yourself getting upset, ask yourself:

1)   What is the problem?

2)   What options do I have to deal with it? List all your choices.

3)   What are the consequences of each of these options?

4)   What is the best choice?

5)   What did I do?

6)   How did that go? Did I make a good decision? How did others feel?

7)   What will I do next time?

| | |
|---|---|
| What is the problem? | Someone keeps getting in my way when I'm trying to run onto my skateboard for a jump. |
| What are the options? | 1) Scream at them. <br> 2) Hit them. <br> 3) Call them names. <br> 4) Tell them firmly to stop (making sure they know why). "You're getting in my way. I'm getting really frustrated and you're making me not want to play with you." <br> 5) Move away and find a different run up space. |
| What are the consequences? | 1, 2 and 3 – I get in trouble. Other kids are uncomfortable with my behaviour and don't want to be friends. Parents are upset with my behaviour and don't want their kids to play with me in case they copy me. I regret how I dealt with it. <br><br> 4) They might stop. If they don't I can move away or ask an adult to help. <br><br> 5) I have a space to do my run up. If they follow me and continue I can find an adult to help. I know in my heart that I did the right thing. |

| | |
|---|---|
| What did I do? | I told them to stop (but forgot to be specific about why), then asked an adult for help. |
| How did that go? | I felt good because they stopped running in front of my board and I dealt with it pretty well. The other kids were comfortable and happy playing with me and wanted to be friends. |
| What will I do next time? | I would do that again but I would be more specific in telling them why I wanted them to stop. |

# NOW IT'S YOUR TURN

It might seem easy to problem-solve when you follow these questions, but to be able to do it quickly when you're right in the middle of a situation you need to …

## PRACTISE     PRACTISE     PRACTISE

## Superhero toolbox 2

### Problem-solving practise

Here are some examples of problems you can use. You could come up with a real problem that happened in your day or choose one from the following list. You can write out answers or talk it through with someone who cares about you.

- A kid at school knocks paint onto your picture.

- Your dad asks you to do the dishes and you don't want to.

- Your little sister breaks your Lego building.

- You've lost your favourite game.

- Someone gets in your way on the playground.

- Your mum asks you to go to bed and you're not feeling tired.

- You're playing a game and losing.

- You've been told to come off your iPad when you're in the middle of a game.

Answer these questions to learn how to solve problems.

| What is the problem? | |
| --- | --- |
| What are the options? | |
| What are the consequences? | |
| What did I do? | |
| How did that go? | |
| What will I do next time? | |

Another way to problem-solve is to get in early and do some pre-planning. If you know there are some situations that often upset you, jot down some ideas and solutions beforehand. Now you have a plan for the next time it happens rather than having to think on the spot. You can make a mind map or make it more interesting with a bug map like this:

**I can do these**                    **I can say these (firmly but respectfully)**

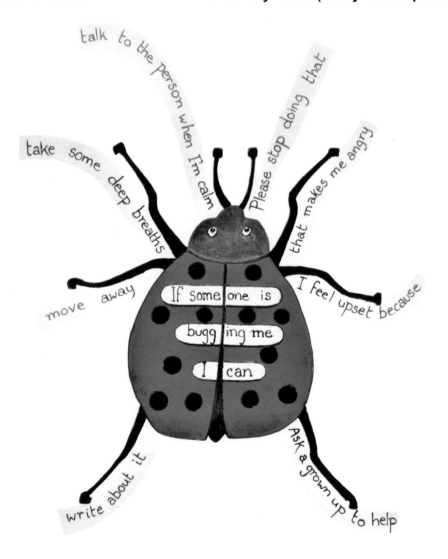

# Chapter 5

## Positive Self-talk

The words you say to yourself without speaking are called **self-talk**.

If something is upsetting, maybe school work is too hard or something happens in the playground, you have 2 choices.

You can say something negative to yourself, which is only going to make you feel worse. Your mind says, 'this is too hard, this is so unfair, this is the worst day ever.'

This is **NEGATIVE SELF-TALK.**

**OR**

You can say something positive to yourself to stay calm and do your best in the circumstance. Your mind says, 'stay calm, I can do this, I can ask for help if I need it.'

This is **POSITIVE SELF-TALK**.

I can do this          I can do this          **I CAN** do this

Some people call negative self-talk their 'thought monster'. You can tame it and feel better and calmer by swapping in positive self-talk when you notice the negative thoughts creeping in.

Everyone has negative self-talk sometimes. The more you practise positive self-talk, the more automatic it becomes.

*'Life is 10% what happens to you and 90% how you respond to it.'*
*(Charles R Swindoll)*

Look at our ideas to challenge negative thoughts in **superhero toolbox 3**. Think about the common negative thoughts that can get in your way and come up with some positive ideas you can use instead. It's really helpful to do this with someone who cares about you, so that you can share ideas.

# Superhero toolbox 3

Positive self-talk ideas: What can I say to myself? What would I say to a friend?

| Negative thoughts | Swap in the positive thoughts |
|---|---|
| I'm no good at this. I give up. | <ul><li>I'm finding this hard but I need to keep trying.</li><li>I'll practise more. I'll get it.</li><li>I can ask for help if I need it.</li><li>I can calm down.</li></ul> |
| This is the worst day ever. | <ul><li>There will be some good in this day. I need to notice the good things too and use my positive self-talk.</li><li>I've solved problems before.</li><li>I'll feel happier in a little while.</li></ul> |
| I've made a mistake. | <ul><li>Everyone makes mistakes. I can learn from this.</li></ul> |
| I'm always in trouble. | <ul><li>Everyone gets in trouble sometimes. I can learn from this and make good choices next time.</li></ul> |
| Everyone teases me.<br><br>No one likes me. | <ul><li>Everyone gets teased sometimes.</li><li>Not everyone will like me but I have family and friends who know me well and like me.</li></ul> |
| It's their fault that I'm in trouble. | <ul><li>I've made a mistake. I need to fix it.</li></ul> |

Now fill in your own positive self-talk ideas that you can say to yourself.

# Calm for Kids

| Negative thought | Alternative positive thought |
|---|---|
|  |  |
|  |  |
|  |  |
|  |  |
|  |  |
|  |  |

# Thinking Errors

There are some common thinking 'traps' we can fall into which may make us feel worse than we need to. Have you noticed that you fall into these 'traps'? If you learn to recognize that this is happening, you can use your positive self-talk to give those thinking errors a superhero 'zap'!

## All or nothing thinking

Black and white thinking. Things are all good or all bad rather than shades of grey. 'If I can't win I won't play the game.'

## Catastrophising

Thinking the worst or exaggerating/making things out to be worse than they are.

## Minimising

Down-playing the positives.

## Mind reading

Thinking that you know what other people are thinking – 'they think I'm stupid.'

## Filtering

Noticing the negative, ignoring the positive.

## Labelling

'I'm an idiot.' 'They're idiots.' It's not accurate thinking and ignores all good points.

## Assuming something is about you

If someone we know ignores us on the street, assuming that they are mad with us when a simple explanation is that maybe they haven't seen us.

## Emotional reasoning

Thinking how you feel is a fact, no matter what the evidence. 'I feel that they don't like me, so I know they don't.'

## Overgeneralising

Assuming because one thing happened it will be true of all similar occasions. 'I didn't get into the sports team. It means that I never will because I'm not good at sport.' 'That person with blue eyes was rude to me. It means blue-eyed people are rude.'

## Unfair expectations

Unfairly comparing ourselves with others who may have achieved more but may have had lucky breaks or more support. This ruins our motivation.

## Blaming

Holding someone else responsible for something negative that has happened, maybe when you're not really sure or even when you were the one involved. 'It's not my fault I forgot my PE gear. Mum didn't pack it for me. It's so unfair. I always get the blame.'

A bit more about that blaming … isn't it better if things aren't my fault?

## PROS OF BLAMING

Seems like you're going to avoid taking responsibility and avoid getting into trouble.

## CONS OF BLAMING

It makes you feel angrier.

It makes you feel stink about your character.

It makes you lose friends.

You get into trouble (people don't like it when someone repeatedly blames others when things go wrong).

# Chapter 6

## Impulsive behaviour

Some people can sit quietly and focus all day, but for others this isn't so easy. It can be really tough to sit down and keep quiet in class when we need to, especially if it's hard or boring. Sometimes we can feel the urge to call out, make a joke or run around.

At the right time (like playtime), these behaviours can be a really important way to have fun and 'let off steam'. But there are times when that same behaviour is not expected.

When a behaviour is unexpected it might make people laugh but it also can make them feel uncomfortable or not want to be around the person doing it. They might have thoughts like, 'she's calling out again, I can't concentrate', or the teacher might think, 'I've worked really hard preparing this lesson but I can't help children learn when someone keeps distracting the class.'

Some people call this unexpected behaviour 'impulsiveness'. You might have heard other descriptions like 'silly,' or the one we like best, 'spontaneous'.

Being spontaneous can be a really good thing because people who are, can often think quickly - and it's thought to be linked to creativity and curiosity.

But if the same behaviour is getting you into trouble in class or making it tough to keep friends, you might find that it's making life challenging. It can be really hard to just stop these behaviours too.

For some people, noticing their feelings can help. If we're excited, tense or wound up, using strategies to calm down can help us to make good decisions.

However, some kids can try REALLY HARD to stop impulsive/spontaneous behaviour (when it's not the right time), but it isn't enough. They might need extra support or even medication and that is OK.

Make a start on **worksheet 4** to help you to understand what can trigger impulsive or spontaneous behaviour and then have a go at our 'superhero strategies' to see if they can help.

## Worksheet 4

## Triggers

What are my triggers for behaving in an impulsive or spontaneous way at an unexpected time? The teacher saying something I could make a joke out of.

Other people calling out in class. Lots of noise or distractions.

What do I look like when I'm
feeling impulsive?

What do I think when
I'm being impulsive?

What does my body feel like
when I'm feeling impulsive?

What might others feel/think when I'm
being impulsive at an unexpected time?

- 
- 
- 
- 
- 
- 
-

# Pros and cons of your behaviour

If your feelings have calmed down and you have stayed in control, but you're not sure what decision you should make, then making a list of the pros and cons can help.

That's a fancy way of saying list the good things about the decisions... **and** the not so good things. This strategy actually can be useful if you find yourself struggling to make a decision for any reason. Here's an example.

Will I keep trying to make a joke out of what the teacher says in class?

## Pros

- It makes the other kids laugh.

- I feel less bored.

- It gives me a buzz (a little excited feeling).

## Cons

- Calling out and cracking a joke is not an expected behaviour in class.

- It makes other kids feel uncomfortable and not want to be friends.

- I could get a reputation as 'the naughty kid'.

- Parents don't want their kids to play with me.

- The teacher feels angry or hurt. They worked hard on their lesson plan and I distracted everyone.

- I get into trouble.

- I feel disappointed in my behaviour.

When you have your decision, come up with a plan and what strategies you will use to make this change.

**For example**: I don't want to keep calling out in class and getting in trouble, so I can try these strategies:

- Notice if I feel excited/tense.

- Take 3 breaths and think 'I can calm down'. See page 13 for **'Turtle breathing'.**

- STOP and T.H.I.N.K. See **toolbox 4.**

- STOP - What will the teacher think? What will the other kids think?

*'You have brains in your head, you have feet in your shoes, you can steer yourself in any direction you choose!'* **Dr Seuss**

# Superhero toolbox 4

This is the T.H.I.N.K strategy to help you make great decisions if you feel REALLY over excited.

It can also be useful if we feel angry.

Is my decision? …

**T**houghtful

**H**elpful

**I**nspiring

**N**ecessary

**K**ind

Because there is no rewind button in life.

Learn to see the bigger picture.

If something is upsetting to us, it's easy to lose perspective. Focusing on the bigger picture helps us to respond in a more helpful way. We can do this by thinking:

- What would this look like to someone not in the situation?

- What's the best way to react in this situation?

- What would your parent/caregiver think?

- This feels like a big deal now. But will it matter in an hour? A day? A week? A month? A year?

# Chapter 7

## The Worry Chapter

Worry or 'anxiety' is a normal feeling and everyone feels worried sometimes. It can be a really helpful feeling too.

You may have heard of 'fight or flight' – the response our bodies have that gets us ready to prepare for danger when we feel anxious.

For example, if a bear was chasing you, anxiety helps you to get to safety as quickly as possible - it would not be a good time to feel relaxed! Feeling a little bit anxious before a test can help us to be alert and do our best.

Sometimes we can feel worried or anxious at a time when it is not helpful or we can worry frequently. A lot of people feel anxious quite often and there are 'superhero' strategies they learn to use to manage their feelings – we'll share some with you.

Learning to notice when you feel anxious is a great start. Fill in **worksheet 5** to see what happens in your body when you're anxious, and then you can use your strategies to calm the feelings down. It's important to know that, like anger, feeling worried or anxious can't hurt you. It can be an uncomfortable feeling but it will pass.

We have already learned some strategies to manage anger that can also help when you're worried. One that is SUPER helpful for anxiety is talking about your worries to someone who cares about you.

If no one is around when you need them, using self-talk is a great strategy. If you fill in some common 'worry' thoughts on your worksheet you can write some alternatives to challenge those thoughts when you start to have them again.

**Ask someone who cares about you to help if possible.**

## Worksheet 5

What happens to you when you're worried? Fill in the work sheet to learn more about worry.

What does your face look like?          What things do you say to yourself?

What happens to your body?              What helps to calm you down?

- 
- 
- 
- 
- 
- 

Worry can be a useful feeling. Write down any ideas about how worry can help you.

- 
- 
- 

If there's not a problem that can easily be solved, some relaxation exercises might be really helpful. Here are a few you can try – practice them when you're not feeling worried.

# Relaxation techniques

If we feel tense, anxious and constantly wound up, some simple techniques can help us to feel more relaxed and calm. These are good to practise at first when we're feeling alright - because this makes it easier to use them when we're not. Some people use these special techniques just to help them fall asleep at night.

## Do not perform any of these actions if they cause any pain

### Progressive Muscle Relaxation

Make yourself comfortable and free of all distractions. Feel the rhythm of your breathing, slowly in and out. Rest your hands on your stomach and notice it moving with each breath.

### Hands

Imagine you have a perfect fluffy pink marshmallow in each hand. Now clench your fists into balls and crush those marshmallows as hard as you can! Feel the tension from your hands all the way up your arms. Wait for 30 seconds and then gradually relax both hands and arms. Notice the difference in how your muscles feel now.

### Shoulders

Once your arms have recovered, stretch them both high above and behind your head until you feel a strong pull in both shoulders. Imagine you're trying to pick the highest apple off a tree. Keep up this stretch for 30 seconds, pushing even a bit higher if possible. Then let your arms flop back to the resting position. Keep noticing how your body feels when it relaxes back.

## Neck

Now imagine you have a walnut on each shoulder. Then raise your shoulders up towards both ears and feel your head pushing down into your shoulders and try and crack the walnuts between them. Then drop your shoulder down low and relax your head, shoulders and neck. Notice the different feeling in your muscles again

## Jaw

Clench your teeth together for 30 seconds, like you're trying to glue them shut and then stretch your mouth so that it is as wide as you can make it for a further 30 seconds. Then relax your whole mouth and let your jaw drop open in a totally relaxed position.

## Nose and Face

Imagine you are trying to stop yourself sneezing and wrinkle your nose up in as many ways as you possibly can. Hold each wrinkle position for a few seconds then relax.

## Stomach

Tense your stomach up and imagine it is a hard rock. Hold that feeling for 30 seconds. You may need to take shallower breaths during this action. Then relax, imagining it has turned from a solid rock into a bowl of jelly. This very relaxed sensation will be accompanied by easier breathing and now take some further slow deep breaths in and out.

## Legs and feet

While standing, clench your toes up tightly and imagine you're trying to pick something up from the floor. Then relax your toes and push down hard with both feet, at the same time spreading your toes out. Repeat this a couple of times and then relax.

After completing this progressive muscle relaxation revert back to some slow deep breaths with your hands resting lightly on your stomach and imagine yourself to be in a very calming situation e.g. lying on a beach with your eyes closed, on a windless warm day, with the sound of gentle waves lapping at the shore.

It's great to practise this a few times and then you can use it when you feel tense, worried, or if you have trouble falling asleep at night.

## Cloud relaxation

When you are at the end of your muscle relaxation keep your eyes closed and continue to be aware of your gentle breathing.

Then start to notice how light your body is feeling, starting with your toes and gradually working your way up your body until you feel as if you are as light as a leaf, floating slowly up towards the clouds. Then you feel the clouds wrap round you as you pass above them into the warmth of the sun.

Rest there for a few moments.

Then be aware of a heaviness gradually making its way up your body and you are slowly falling back down to earth. Lower and lower until you gently land back on the ground. But the ground gives way under your weight and you start sinking through the earth, deeper and deeper.

Then, once again, there is a gradual return of that feeling that you are getting lighter and lighter and you float up to the surface and the whole cycle of rise and fall continues.

After repeating this a few times, when you come back to earth, resting, gently breathing, notice how relaxed all your muscles feel.

## Mindfulness

Sometimes we can get so caught up in worrying about what might happen, or thinking about what has happened, that we don't pay attention to what is happening right now. Taking a few simple breaths and focusing on our senses - what we can hear, see, smell and taste - can help us to feel calm. Here's an exercise that can help you ...

Sitting in a chair, close your eyes. Take 5 slow breaths in and out, noticing your stomach rising and falling with each breath. When you have finished, notice your body. What do your feet feel like on the floor? Can you feel your body sitting in the chair? Are your hands resting on your legs? Now turn your attention to the outside. What sounds can you hear? What can you see?

This exercise can take less than a minute and has been shown to help people to feel calm and even to improve some medical conditions.

# Chapter 8

## Friendship Skills

## Worksheet 6

Some people seem to think it's easy to make friends. Sometimes it just seems to happen and other times it takes more effort and maybe a little luck.

If you think about friendship, what do you think makes a good friend? What sort of a friend would you like to be?

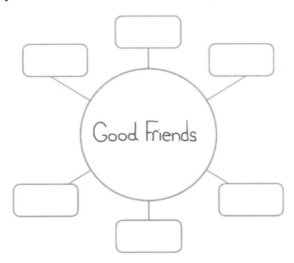

**Some ideas**

- Reliable
- Shares
- Supports me when I am sad
- Uses kind language
- Good listener
- Spends fun time together
- Apologises for mistakes
- Works together to solve problems

## Superhero toolbox 5

### Saying sorry and repairing mistakes

Saying sorry is SUPER important. It's hard for a friendship (or any relationship) to last if you make a mistake and don't try to repair it.

The apology must be genuine, even if you need a few moments to calm down and think about it first. A dishonest apology can be more hurtful and damaging.

There are four simple steps you can follow to help you make a great apology.

1) I'm sorry that I …

2) I shouldn't have done that because …

3) Next time I will …

4) Is there anything I can do to help you feel better …

Go up to the person, face them and make eye contact.

This sounds like a lot of work

## How do I know all this practise is worth the effort?

PRACTISE     PRACTISE     PRACTISE!

This picture is a slice of your brain. The fluffy outside bits are your neurons and the stringy bits are your axons. Axons are the pathways which carry messages through your brain.

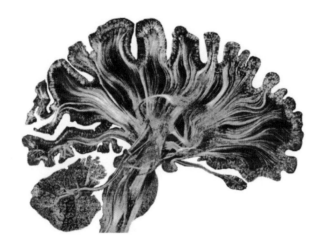

Every time you practise positive thinking or any of these strategies, you strengthen those pathways and help to make those new thoughts and behaviours automatic.

If you forget to, even thinking afterwards, 'how would I do that next time', will help strengthen those pathways.

It's the same thing that happens when you exercise. If you practise lifting weights over and over again, the muscles in your arms would get bigger and stronger.

# Chapter 9

## What I like about me

If things are getting you down, make sure you don't forget all your best parts. It can be easy to do this, but then you're being tricked by one of the 'thinking errors' on page 28. Can you remember which one it is? That's right, **filtering**, noticing the negative and ignoring the positive. Remembering what's great about you, your dreams and goals and even thinking about people you admire, can really help you to feel better. Fill in **worksheet 6** and you can ask someone who cares about you for ideas if you need help.

Work sheet 6: What are my best bits?

Examples:

- Great sense of humour, creative, caring, active.

- Generous, loyal, loves to learn, doesn't give up easily.

**What are my goals?**

Take some time to think about what excites you in your life and what goals you would like to achieve. These ideas may change from day to day but some will keep coming in to your mind. They may be to do with sport, relationships, adventure, media and what you would hope to be when you grow up.

Add your own ideas to the graphic below.

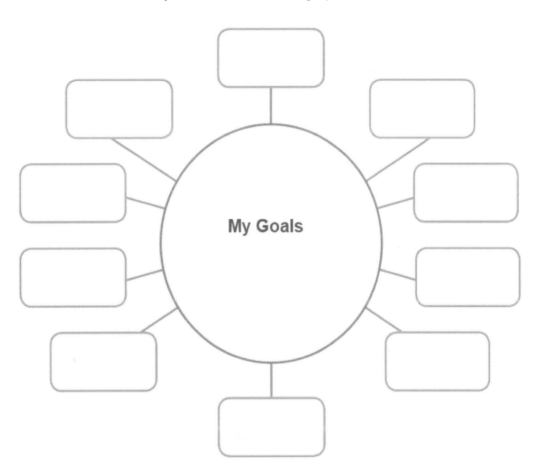

# My Notes

## References and recommended reading:

A number of experts have been the source of ideas and provided guidance which has contributed significantly to the writing of this book. Additional recommended readings and references include the following:

**The Incredible Years**: A Trouble-Shooting Guide for Parents of Children Aged 2-8 Years. Paperback – January 1 2006 Carolyn Webster-Stratton

**The Zones of Regulation**: Created by Leah M Kuypers 2011

**The Optimistic Child**: Martin Seligman Paperback May 2 2011

**The Explosive Child**. A new approach for parenting and understanding easily frustrated children.  Ross W Greene  Paperback  May 1 2014

Denson, T.F., (2015). Four promising psychological interventions for reducing reactive aggression. *Current Opinion in Behavioral Sciences. 3,* 136-141, https://doi.org/10.1016/j.cobeha.2015.04.003.

Klingbeil, D. A., Fischer, A. J., Renshaw, T. L., Bloomfield, B. S., Polakoff, B.,Willenbrink, J. B., and Chan, K. T. (2017). Effects of mindfulness-based interventions on disruptive behaviour: A meta-analysis of single-case research. *Psychology in the Schools*, 54: 70–87. http://dx.doi.org/10.1002/pits.21982.

Lohaus, A. & Klein-Hessling, J. (2003) Relaxation in Children: Effects of Extended and Intensified Training, Psychology & Health, 18:2, 237-249, DOI: 10.1080/0887044021000057257

Macklem, G. L. (2008). *Practitioner's guide to emotion regulation in school-aged children.* Springer Science + Business Media. https://psycnet.apa.org/record/2007-13789-000

Ratcliffe, B., Wong, M., Dossetor, D., & Hayes, S. (2014).

Teaching social–emotional skills to school-aged children with Autism Spectrum Disorder: A treatment versus control trial in 41 mainstream schools. Research in Autism Spectrum Disorders, 8, (12), 1722-1733. https://doi.org/10.1016/j.rasd.2014.09.010.

Rosanbalm, K.D., & Murray, D.W. (2017). Promoting self-regulation in early childhood: A practise Brief. Washington, DC: Office of Planning, Research, and Evaluation. Administration for Children and Families, US. Department of Health and Human Services. https://fpg.unc.edu/sites/fpg.unc.edu/files/resources/reports-and-policy-briefs/PromotingSelf-RegulationIntheFirstFiveYears.pdf

Sukhodolsky, D. G., Smith, S. D., McCauley, S. A., Ibrahim, K., & Piasecka, J. B. (2016). Behavioral Interventions for Anger, Irritability, and Aggression in Children and Adolescents. *Journal of child and adolescent psychopharmacology*, *26*(1), 58–64. https://doi.org/10.1089/cap.2015.0120

Thompson, R.A. (1991). Emotional regulation and emotional development. *Educational Psychology Review*. doi:10.1007/bf01319934

Weare, K. (2013). 'Developing mindfulness with children and young people: a review of the evidence and policy context.' *Journal of Children's Services*, Vol. 8( 2): 141 – 153.

Weare, K. (2018). The evidence for mindfulness in schools for children and young people.

University of Exter. https://ave-institut.de/wp-content/uploads/Weare-Evidence_for_mindfulness_in_schools.pdf

Wyman, P.A., Cross, W., Brown, H,. Yu, Q., Tu, X., & Eberly, S. (2010). Intervention to Strengthen Emotional Self-Regulation in Children with Emerging Mental Health Problems: Proximal Impact on School Behaviour.

*Journal of Abnormal Child Psychology*, 38(5): 707-720.  doi: https://doi.org/10.1007/s10802-010-9398-x

Zoogman, S., Goldberg, S. B., Hoyt, W. T., and Miller, L. (2014). 'Mindfulness interventions with youth: A meta-analysis'. *Mindfulness,* 6(2), 290-302.

# ABOUT THE AUTHORS

## Julie Cullen

Julie is a paediatric physiotherapist with almost 20 years of experience, who has worked for various District Health Boards in New Zealand. She has an interest both in this topic, and in supporting children and their whānau to thrive.

## Steve Connellan

Steve is a retired hospital consultant physician. He worked in the UK NHS for 35 years. He has published research in peer reviewed journals, books on art and medical topics. In retirement he has had the opportunity to publish illustrated children's stories in verse for his grandchildren.

Printed in Great Britain
by Amazon

39518857R00034